Baby Boy

A Mother's Story

Marilyn Pelkey

iUniverse

BABY BOY
A MOTHER'S STORY

iUniverse books may be ordered through booksellers or by contacting:

iUniverse LLC
1663 Liberty Drive
Bloomington, IN 47403
www.iuniverse.com
1-800-Authors (1-800-288-4677)

Because of the dynamic nature of the Internet, any web addresses or
links contained in this book may have changed since publication and
may no longer be valid. The views expressed in this work are solely those
of the author and do not necessarily reflect the views of the publisher,
and the publisher hereby disclaims any responsibility for them.

Any people depicted in stock imagery provided by Thinkstock are
models, and such images are being used for illustrative purposes only.
Certain stock imagery © Thinkstock.

ISBN: 978-1-4917-4370-6 (sc)
ISBN: 978-1-4917-4369-0 (e)

Library of Congress Control Number: 2014917015

Printed in the United States of America.

iUniverse rev. date: 09/30/2014

Dedication

For my Mother who said I should, without your encouragement and support this would not have been possible. For my daughter Beth who gives me strength and my husband Stephen for his patience throughout this journey. For Brendan, Randy and Kira, so you may know your Father, the man that he was and how very much he loved you.

Preface

I have heard it said that we live two lives, one before diagnosis and one after. I find that statement to be very profound, that one sentence describes me perfectly.

When my second life began everything was hard. Going to the grocery store was probably most difficult, I would have panic attacks and not be able to finish my shopping so after a while I stopped going. A year had passed before I had finally went back. I was trying so hard to find my way out of the darkness, most days I just wanted to crawl under the bed with all the dust bunnies and stay there.

Two years into my second life after becoming involved with Relay for Life, I wrote many articles for our local newspaper and well as speeches that I would give at the events. My words always seemed to flow so easily which made the idea of writing down our story seem like the next logical step.

In 2008 while on summer vacation with pen and paper in hand I began a journey that would take me a few years to complete. There were times I would sit and giggle at the memories and there were times when my words seemed to flow effortlessly and before I realized it I would have several pages written. There were also many sections that were just too painful and I would have to put it aside for a while, sometimes months would go by before I would pick it up again. In the end this process has been very cathartic, while I would be perfectly content to still be living my first life I like who I am now. I believe I am a stronger person and more willing to take on new challenges.

My heart and soul have gone into the following pages so for those who take the time to read my story who are like me, living your second life, I hope you find comfort in the knowledge that you are not alone. For my family and friends the following is the reason why the person I was no longer exists, Thank you for loving the person I have become.

Introduction

I used to love summer; not so much anymore. It has taken on a whole new meaning; all of the different scents conjure too many memories.

Three years. I've been so busy concentrating on taking baby steps that I find it hard to believe three years has passed. It all still seems like yesterday. Many things can happen in three years: baby girls becoming big girls with missing teeth, little boys becoming young men with changing voices and hairy legs.

Most days, when I look in the mirror, I don't recognize the woman staring back. She has lines on her face that weren't there before, and her eyes look so sad. I'm not the same person I was three years ago. None of us are. You can't go through what we did and not be changed by it.

My daughter Elizabeth has taken steps to move forward with her life and get things back on track. She will still tell you, "I have issues," but I'm so proud of her for the strength she has shown and the challenges she has taken on. She has been my rock and I thank God every day for her.

I believe I'm a stronger person today. Some of the things I have done in the last couple of years, I never would have done even five years ago, one of them being public speaking. For someone who was terrified to give oral book reports in school, this is quite a feat.

Three years. Summer, August, I'm so tired, and not just because I'm back to not sleeping. I'm tired of people saying, "Yes, but you're okay, it's been three years." I'll never be okay. I'm simply learning to live with my new reality.

I remember saying to my mom early on that I know I'm not the first, and I won't be the last, but in my heart it feels like I'm the only.

Sometimes, when speaking with my parents, I still lie and tell them I'm doing fine. I really just don't want them to worry. Yet other times when they ask, all I can do is cry. I have, however, taken steps to help myself and my family by becoming involved in a worthy cause, in trying to ensure that the time we do spend together as a family is quality time and just by trying to become a happier me. And finally, I've decided to write down our story.

This story has become a very important part of the history of my family. My hope is not only that it will help them and bring them some comfort and peace, but that it will do the same for anyone who reads this. One of the lines I use in my speeches is, "Our stories are all different, but they are all the same."

Chapter 1

I grew up in a small town in New Brunswick. You know the one; if you blink you'll miss it? Well, that's the one. I grew up as one of six children, which meant that there was always someone to play with, although don't get me wrong, we sometimes fought more than we played.

We lived at the foot of a mountain, so in winter months we didn't have far to go tobogganing. We weren't allowed to go all the way to the top. Of course, being kids, we did anyway and boy, what a ride. We also lived next to the woods and built many camps. The name of the camps was always the same, Hodge Podge LodgeHome of the Outsiders, we were the outsiders.

Most Sundays were spent at my maternal grandmother's, with many aunts, uncles and cousins. I have many fond memories of playing Red Rover, Mother May I and Giant Steps. When family would come from Ontario for a visit, these Sundays were filled with music, as most of my family play guitar and sing.

We never knew, growing up, that Mom and Dad had to struggle to make ends meet, or that Mom wished she could have given us more. As far as we knew, we had everything we needed. The Christmas tree was always surrounded by a mountain of gifts, we always got something nice for our birthdays and home was a safe, warm place where we all felt loved and nothing bad ever happened.

I was always in such a hurry to grow up to meet someone, fall in love and have babies of my own; to have what my parents did. I remember going through the Eaton's catalogue, cutting out pictures of all the beautiful babies and pretending I was their 'mommy.' My parents naturally tried to get all of us to slow down. We all grow up soon enough, and childhood lasts such a short time, but what teenager listens to their parents? And girls, we romanticize everything.

I started dating my husband Stephen when I was only sixteen, he was nineteen. We were both so young but I knew he was the right man for me. It wasn't long and I became pregnant so we decided to get married. I remember when we told my parents we were both so terrified; my Dad simply said "it's no bed of roses!' Truer words have never been spoken, marriage is hard work but when you love someone in the end it's worth it.

All the while I was pregnant I knew I was carrying a boy. We didn't have ultra sounds in 1976 like they do today so there was no way to confirm my suspicions. However I just knew, his name would be Shane Stephen.

Kendall was born on May 27, 1976; he weighed 6 lbs 11½ oz. Yes that's right, I said Kendall. I took one look at him and thought *Oh, you are not a Shane.* I started looking through baby books for a suitable name, we had already decided his second name would be Graydon after an Uncle of my husbands who had been killed in a train accident on April 1st of that year. We finally decided on Kendall, it means chief of the valley; I liked that and thought he would grow up to be a leader. Like every mom I had great expectations.

At that time, we lived across the street from my in-laws. When Kendall was old enough, as in able to walk and turn a door knob, he would sneak out to go and have breakfast with his grandfather. Shirt on inside out, pants on backwards, boots on the wrong feet, away he would go. My husband and I tried everything. We put a chain lock on the door, he used a broom handle to slide it over. We put a table in front of the door, he would crawl under it. He always managed to escape to have breakfast with Grampy, pretty smart for a two-year-old. After a while, we gave up and I'm glad we did. All of those early mornings spent with his grandparents became special memories for all three of them.

Kendall's two favorite playmates were his cousins Heidi and Lindsay. They were only a few months older than Kendall, but couple that with being girls and, as you can imagine, Kendall played house a lot. For Christmas the year that he was two, Santa brought Kendall a doll of his own. My mom knit a little boy outfit for him, and Kendall named him Danny. That doll is still in the family. In fact, Kendall's children all played with him and he is at present in a toy box in my basement. Even though Kendall's two cousins had him playing house, he was always all boy. His hero was the Incredible Hulk, and his favorite pastime pounding nails into a block of wood. The latter, an aunt of my husband's discovered while she was watching him for me. They were doing some renovating, and Kendall decided to help.

Family get-togethers were still a very important part of our lives, so Kendall was always surrounded by people who loved him. One weekend, when Kendall was two, we were planning to have a potluck at my parents' house on Sunday, so I decided to make a coconut cream pie on Saturday evening. I took it out of the oven, placed it on the kitchen table and went to bed. When I got up Sunday morning, there was Kendall, standing on a chair and throwing pie all over my kitchen. He was coconut cream from one end of him to the other, grinning from ear to ear. I just stood there in shocked silence for a few moments. The meringue was stuck to my kitchen curtains, not to mention that there wasn't even a clean path on the floor to get to him. He looked at me, giggled, picked up more pie filling and threw it my way. In the years to come, I often reminded him of that moment. Not that he would have any clear memory of it himself, as he was so young at the time. I don't recall what I made to take to the potluck that day, but I do have a very clear picture of my beautiful two-year-old son covered in coconut cream, having a great time redecorating my kitchen.

Throughout my life, I have often thought how cool it would be to see the future, like a fortune teller. Now, looking back at this moment and picturing my little boy's face, eyes bright with laughter, face beaming through gobs of coconut cream, I'm glad I didn't know what was to come. I'm glad that ability was just the fantasy of a young woman.

Shortly before Kendall's fourth birthday, my husband and I decided to move west. That was such a tough decision, but my husband felt there was no future for him there. Leaving our families was hard. Taking Kendall away from his home - the people he loved and who loved him - was harder. This is one of my many regrets. I often say, "All well, choices that we make," in reference to a lot of life's ups and downs and I do believe this to be true. Therefore, I believe that one should have no regrets. This particular regret, however, is not for me but for my son. He had no choice. He was only four years old. My regret is that he grew up without grandparents and cousins, aunts and uncles. Although we made the trip home several times, there's nothing like having all of your family close-by and knowing they will be there for birthdays and concerts and Christmas, and all those special moments in a child's life.

Kendall never forgot his New Brunswick roots, and always felt a strong connection not just to the people, but to the province, and he always, always considered it home.

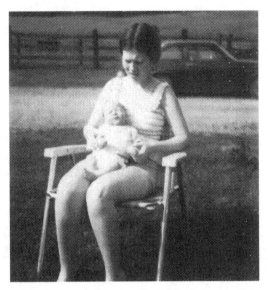

Kendall and I, one month old.

*Kendall and Heidi playing together before
we moved to Saskatchewan.*

Chapter 2

In May of 1980, we made the move to Saskatchewan. Being the outgoing and likeable little boy that he was, it didn't take long for Kendall to make friends with all the children in our neighborhood. We rented a house on a corner lot, and across the street was a paddling pool, complete with lifeguards. Kendall called it *his* pool, and he was so excited when it opened for the season.

Kendall and I both found those first few months difficult. We missed being with our family back east. Every time I spoke with my parents or siblings, most of the conversation consisted of me crying and Kendall saying, "Can I talk?"

Being all boy, Kendall played hard all day, so after his evening bath it became our routine to snuggle on the couch together watching TV. I would rub his head and stroke his hair, and if I stopped he would take my hand and move it back so that I would keep going. He never outgrew this. Through all his childhood illnesses or any time he just needed his mom to comfort him - and then of course later on in his life - this old routine would resurface.

In December of 1981, we gave Kendall a sister named Elizabeth. I finally had my baby girl and what a beauty, all soft and pink with a head of beautiful brown curls, in sharp contrast to Kendall's white-blond hair., the perfect family. Beth was born on December the 5th, just a few days before Kendall's first Christmas concert. I knew I would be in the hospital so like any good mom; I picked out an outfit for him to wear as I wanted him to look his best. After the concert Stephen and Kendall came to visit us, in he walked all smiles wearing, yes you guess it play clothes, jeans with a hole in the knee and a faded flannel shirt. I was so thankful that his teacher was aware of our current situation and that his outfit was his father's doing and not mine.

Winter was very peaceful and quiet. During the day it was just Beth and I at home, after school; if she was awake Kendall would sit and talk with her while I made supper. In the evening Kendall would curl up in the rocker with Beth and I and we would read stories, I loved all those moments. As Beth grew so did their relationship he loved to make her laugh and giggle and would spend time everyday rolling around on the floor and making funny faces before going off to play with his friends. Beth was such a good baby by the time she was four months old she would eat for the last time at seven in the evening then off to bed, she would not wake up till seven the next morning. This left enough time in the evening for a television show or a card game or reading some of the books he loved.

When summer finally arrived my husband and I borrowed a tent trailer from a friend and took the kids on a camping trip to Echo Lake. The first night we were there it rain so hard we were stuck in the camper. It had two beds, Kendall was laying on one while Stephen sat on the side facing me, and Beth was rolling around behind me on the bed I sat on. I asked Stephen if she could roll out and he kept saying no the canvas was attached, just now out she went, I caught her little arm as Stephen raced for the door, it took only seconds for him to get her back inside the safety of the camper, she was all smiles with rain drops running off her nose. She ended up on the same bed as Kendall to play until we were all ready for bed. The next day was lovely and warm; after we had breakfast we headed for the beach, sandwiches and drinks in hand. We spent most of the day playing in the water and making sandcastles. All in all it turned out to be a very nice long weekend and the first of many camping trips.

Chapter 3

In May of 1983, we were on the move again, but this time we didn't have as far to go. We moved from the city to a small town about 50 kilometers east of Regina called Indian Head. This would remain our home for the next twenty years. Having the personality that he did, it wasn't long before Kendall made many friends, and of course little girlfriends. Coming from a close and loving family, with Sunday dinners and family picnics at the lake, I naturally wanted to create and give all those same things to my children, even though it was just the four of us. A lot of the things my parents did when I was young, I did with my children and, oddly enough, they carried those traditions with them as they became adults with children of their own. I love how that works.

Kendall liked his new school and his teachers. He did well in school. As his mom, I wished he had done better but he was more interested in sports, which he was always good at. He loved track and field, especially running. There was another boy in his class who always came in first place, Kendall second, so his goal was to beat this boy one day. It wasn't until high school that his goal was realized, and he beamed for days. Softball, baseball, slow pitch, yes, Kendall played them all. He played softball in elementary school; I believe he was in Grade 6 the year I got to coach. In high school, he played fastball. He was the pitcher. It always amazed me, and I felt so proud, the way he would strike out batter after batter. I remember during one game, the coach from the other team tried to get him off the mound, and he just stood there smiling and was allowed to continue. Next would be slow-pitch. My husband, Kendall and Elizabeth all played on the same team. I can't run, catch or throw, so I didn't play. Stephen played second base, and Kendall was shortstop. People referred to it as the Pelkey line, and nothing could get through.

Then there was football. Not a sport I understand, although I do enjoy watching the Saskatchewan Roughriders. In Grade 9, before he was even old enough to be eligible to play on the team, Kendall begged the coach to let him. His persistence, and of course his charming personality, paid off. The coach let him practice with the team, and during the games he acted as the water boy. He started playing in Grade 10, but it wasn't until his senior year that I actually started going to the games. The other boys were bigger and I didn't want to see my boy on the bottom of a pile. Football was such an important part of his life, and I decided that since it was his last year, I should go and support him. And yes, I enjoyed it. I remember during one game in particular, he was running down the field with the ball, being chased by a few big bruisers. None of them could catch him. This one young man made a huge dive at Kendall, and all he came away with was his shoe. Touchdown!

Then there was hockey. My sweet baby boy, who had snuggled with me on the couch watching television while I stroked his hair, who had played on the floor with his baby sister, wanted to play hockey. I'm sure I was being overprotective, but he was ten years old before he was finally allowed to play. Over the next few years, Elizabeth became a "rink rat," and Kendall accumulated a box full of trophies and medals. His Player of the Game trophy still holds a special place on a shelf in my bedroom. When he received that one, I told him it was mine. He looked at me with one of his now infamous grins because, you see, he knew why. After he scored one of many that game, he looked up at me where I was sitting in the stands and bowed. What a ham! My son, my baby boy.

Chapter 4

As mothers, especially young mothers, we always worry and wonder whether we are doing a good job, whether we are teaching our children all the things they need to become good, kind and caring adults. I do believe that Kendall's years playing sports taught him many good things, like fair play and sportsmanship. He also learned that while winning is awesome and amazing, as cheesy as it sounds, in the end how you played the game is just as meaningful and important.

I got a small glimpse of the man Kendall would become at a very early age. He went to a Grade 6 Christmas dance, and he had a little girlfriend at the time. Before the dance, he took some of his babysitting money, went downtown shopping and bought this really pretty necklace for her. He was so proud of his purchase, and he was certain that she would like it. At this dance, there was one little girl that none of the other boys wanted to dance with, so Kendall did. Little girls being the way they are, his girlfriend broke up with him and gave him back the necklace. When he got home that evening, I asked him how things went and he told me the story. He finished by saying, "But it was her dance too, and she should dance at least once." In that moment my heart was so full I thought it would burst. If this was any indication of the man he would become, then he must be listening, and we must be doing a pretty good job.

As he got a little older, my girlfriends found it unusual and cool that Kendall would hug me or kiss my cheek in their presence. Of course, I loved it. He always took the time to speak with my friends, he was polite and respectful and, of course, he was charming. I remember the day he got his driver's license. He came to where I was working to show me. He was so proud, grinning from ear to ear, and for a moment I thought this was something he just wanted to share with me and then he asked me if he could borrow the car. Too funny!

We had our share of battles throughout his teenage years, and I sometimes wondered whether we would make it out the other side with our relationship still intact. He did things like crawl out his bedroom window, which was on the second floor, to go party with friends. When my husband and I would go out for the evening, we would sometimes leave Kendall to babysit his little sister. We found out much later that while we were away, he would go out with his friends and pay Beth in hockey cards to keep her quiet. She never told on him. We only found out when they were much older and we were all sitting around the dinner table sharing stories of their childhood. The one time we did catch him, he had actually taken her with him, and she was so excited to go. They went out one night to visit a friend who had a pool and MTV. My husband and I came home early from an evening out, and I was terrified to find that my kids were gone, and who do you phone when it's almost midnight? Beth never said anything at the time, most likely because she was only eight, but she felt bad that he got into trouble the one and only time he let her tag along. Today she has a collection of hockey cards that brings back fond memories, even though she spent many evenings alone huddled in her parents' bedroom.

All through those difficult years I would say to him, "Kendall, you are my heart," at least once every day. He must have been listening. We eventually made it through those years, as most families do, and he became the kind, caring, gentle man I knew he would be. He also became my dance partner, since I'm pretty sure his dad has two left feet. We started going to the local bar for karaoke, and we would sing songs like "Paradise by the Dashboard Light." People around us were always amazed by the close relationship we had, and the fact that he enjoyed spending time with his mom and her friends. I don't think we ever saw our relationship as unique or different. It was just how we were, and who we were.

Kendall, Beth, and I with Mom her first trip to Saskatchewan.

Kendall and Beth boxing......

I think she won!

Stephen and Kendall showing off their moves.

Kendall and Beth with their Maternal Grandparents
and cousins, Christmas 1989.

Chapter 5

K endall started dating Shelley when he was in Grade 11. I always knew he was a lot like his mother, but I never thought he would follow so closely in my footsteps as to become a parent at the age of 17.

Brendan was born in November of 1993, and what a joy. Once Kendall finished school they rented a small house only a few blocks from where we lived. I would, on a regular basis go over for a visit then take Brendan back to our house for supper. He loved to read stories and sing songs, and Stephen and I loved having him with us. In February of 1996, along came Randy, so very different from his brother. By this time Kendall and Shelley had moved to McLean, a 25 minute drive from Indian Head, so we didn't get to spend as much time with him as we did Brendan, who would come for weekend visits without his parents often. Randy on the other hand only came for visits with his parents. This was very disheartening for my husband and I, we felt that we couldn't develop as strong of bond with Randy like we had with Brendan.

In July of that same year Kendall and Shelley got married. The ceremony was quite lovely and intimate. It took place in the church Shelley and her family attended, afterwards we all went to her parent's farm for the reception. My parents and my sister Anna Marie with her two children came west for the event. Kendall was so happy to have them there as this was the first time extended family were present for an important moment in his life.

A couple weeks later Kendall and Shelley were invited to a wedding in Indian Head so they asked us if we could watch Randy and of course we said yes. As I said we didn't have as strong of bond with Randy so needless to say he screamed and cried for hours. He was so little at the time only 5 months old, I tried everything, I sang to him, we walked and we rocked, I read stories, nothing worked. My husband and I felt so bad, we didn't want to ruin their evening out. In the end they did cut their evening short, they came home around 10:30 with news we had not heard. Princess Diana had been killed in a horrific car crash. We immediately turned on the television, such a horrible tragedy we spent the next hour watching all the updates while Randy quietly slept in his mother's arms.

Kendall and Shelley eventually bought a house across the street from us, and I was thrilled. We had a fire pit in our back yard, so most summer evenings that's where we would be, just hanging out and talking. I remember, when Randy was little, as soon as the stars were out, he always wanted to go inside. It took us a while to figure out why, but it was because of the stars. He didn't understand what was holding them up, and if they were going to fall he didn't want them to land on him.

Kendall and Shelley both traveled to the city Monday through Friday, so my husband and I would pick the boys up from day care. I always considered this our special time. Kendall and Shelley would say I was spoiling them, but I loved my new role as grandmother, and I would just smile at them and say, "It's my job, and I'm good at it."

The boys were always so appreciative of everything we gave them. One time I bought them 'big boy' underwear, and you would have thought I had given them the moon. Randy wasn't quite potty trained at that time, and he took the little underpants out of the pack, checked them out, folded them up and put them back in the pack over and over again, smiling all the while.

Brendan was always my gentle little man, so much like his father. He loved to sit and snuggle and read stories or watch movies. Randy always had to be busy and on the move, playing with little cars, building with Lego or doing puzzles. Those were such happy years. As in every family, there were some trying times, but I don't wish to focus on those memories. I would rather look back at times like when Kendall and Shelley bought a new barbeque. Shelley was working an evening shift and Kendall was making supper for the boys. He ran over to our house in a panic. "Oh my God, Dad, Shelley is going to kill me you have to help me!" As it turns out, Kendall had put the meat on the barbeque, gone inside to check on the potatoes, he had placed the barbeque too close to the house and when he went back outside, the siding was on fire and melting. Luckily, Stephen found some siding that was a perfect match, and they replaced the damaged boards. Shelley would have been none the wiser, except for two very excited little boys.

Shelley worked most Saturdays, so it was up to Kendall and the boys to do the housework. I would phone or visit, and AC/DC or Metallica would be playing loudly. The boys would tidy the living room while Kendall did the kitchen, all of them singing and dancing. It wasn't long before my husband and I were on the move again, next stop, Grenfell. I remember joking with my mom that if we kept moving 50 kilometers east every few years, eventually we would be home. This was another difficult move, leaving all my friends and co-workers, the home in which I raised my children, and of course Kendall and his family. I know 50 kilometers isn't far, but we all get so busy in our daily lives that those 50 kilometers can sometimes feel like hundreds.

Kendall and Shelley gave us a beautiful granddaughter, Kira, in August of 2001. When I first saw Kira, Shelley had her on the couch in their living room. I hurried across the room, so excited to meet my first granddaughter. She was so tiny and sweet. However, I was surprised to see that she was a lovely shade of blue, with this huge curl right on top of her head. Shelley said, "Isn't she beautiful?" and all I could do was laugh; to me she looked like a Smurf. According to the doctors, she came out too fast, and the bruising would soon fade. Even though she looked like a

Smurf it was love at first sight. By this time Stephen was already working in Grenfell. We had spent so much time living apart over the years, I had decided to watch for job postings in that community but until a position became available I would spend my days off travelling there so we could be together. There was one particular week I opted to stay at home since my house work was being neglected. September 11th was a beautiful warm day, I woke up and put on the coffee as usual and went to my computer to say good morning to my sister Anna Marie. She had computers in her class room for her students so we got in the habit of chatting every morning. I typed in *Good morning sis*, her response startled me "Oh my God Marilyn, aren't you watching the news?" Well no I said "I haven't even had my coffee yet." She then typed "oh Marilyn a plane just crashed into one of the twin towers" I quickly ran to the television and put on Canada AM. I just stood there frozen, watching in horror as the events unfolded. I phoned Stephen crying, not sure if they were aware of what was happening. The whole day was so surreal watching all the news coverage in disbelief, so many lives lost. I spent the day going back and forth from our house to Kendall and Shelley's needing to be with my grandchildren and holding Kira who was only five weeks old, needing to believe that there was still good in the world. I held on to the newspapers to one day show Kira, so she could see the tragic events that took place when she was so young.

In October of that year, Grenfell became our new home. Stephen and I were enjoying our new life. Elizabeth was living in Regina, so it was just the two of us. This didn't last long, as Elizabeth soon moved back home. Both Brendan and Randy came for weekend visits, which we enjoyed, and of course we still had regular family dinners.

It was thanks to Elizabeth that Kira came to visit for the first time without her parents or her boys, as she would later refer to Brendan and Randy. Kira was just a little over a year old when Beth stopped to visit the kids on her way home. As she was leaving, Kira toddled over and got her coat, so she could go with her. Beth looked at Kendall and Shelley, who both shrugged their shoulders, so Shelley packed her diaper bag and this would the first of many visits for Kira.

My nickname for Kira, almost immediately, was "Dolly." I loved buying her pretty little outfits and dressing her up. It wasn't long before I bought a sewing machine and taught myself how to make dresses for her. She would come for visits and dress up, put on her princess shoes and crown, and her boys would say, "You know Grammy, she doesn't always have to be so pretty." Sadly, Kendall and Shelley's marriage ended in 2003, and my husband and I had both our children home again.

Kendall would go and pick up the children every weekend and bring them to our home, so we fixed up the basement for them so they could have a place to play and watch movies, and just be together without us always intruding. We enjoyed having them here although, admittedly, sometimes we just wanted our house back. I did love watching Kendall interact with his children, especially Kira. He would say to her, "Who loves you, baby?" and she would respond, "Daddy does!" His nickname for her was "Cheeky Monkey,' she would giggle at this take his hands in hers climb up his body until she could place her small arms around his neck.

This was also an opportunity for Kendall and Elizabeth to become close as young adults. One of the things they did which I, as their mother, found strange was to drive an hour and a half to Regina for burgers. It drove Beth crazy when, after just a few short weeks in Grenfell, Kendall could walk into the local coffee shop or bar, sit at any table and visit with just about anyone. After being here several months, Beth had a close circle of friends and wouldn't have felt comfortable sitting with people she barely knew. Kendall looked at strangers as friends he hadn't met yet. I always admired that about him.

For months, I had hoped that Kendall and Shelley would work things out and get back together. Through late-night conversations with my son, I learned that he wanted the same thing, but this was not to be. My grandmother always used to say that everything in life happens for a reason. It would only be a few short months before the reason for this turn of events became clear. Home is where my baby boy needed to be.

Life is full of twists and turns, ups and downs. Most things like moving halfway across the country, I've always felt are necessary to keep life interesting and shake things up a bit. Sometimes, however, life throws you a giant curve ball that you don't see coming, and you are forever changed by it.

Kendall, Beth and Myself at Kendall's High School Graduation.

Kendall and Beth at their Aunt Debbie's in New Brunswick '95

Dancing with my Baby Boy.

Kendall and Shelley on the Tobique.

Kendall with his boys and Beth at Heidi's wedding.

Kendall with his boys on the walking bridge in Four Falls,
New Brunswick, not far from where I grew up.

Kendall home from work on a Friday, being goofy,
excited to go get the kids for the weekend.

Chapter 6

On a Thursday in 2004, just a few days before Easter, Kendall was diagnosed with cancer. For months, he had been complaining about a medical problem that he was having, but I truly thought from the way he was describing it that he had a hernia. I don't know why. Maybe if he had been more forthcoming but, being a young man, I'm sure he found it difficult to explain fully what was happening. Maybe if he had, or maybe if I had asked more questions. I don't know, another regret.

I was at a work meeting on a Wednesday evening. When I returned home, Kendall was just getting out of the tub. Stephen was down the street visiting with Elizabeth, who had moved out of our home a few months prior.

Kendall started asking me again about this problem he was having, and I could see that he was upset, so I said, "Is it in a place you can show me? Because I just don't have a clear picture of what you're telling me." He had been to the local doctor, who had sent him to a specialist in Regina, and he was on a short wait list for further testing.

This doctor had given him a list of all the things it could be. You just never dream or imagine.

As soon as he showed it to me, my heart sank. I'm not sure whether I knew, or what I knew. I phoned for my husband to come home, and when he asked what was wrong I told him he had to take Kendall to the hospital now. The doctor he saw was more than a little concerned, and Kendall spent the night there. The next day, I went to work as usual and my husband, who was on days off, went to the hospital in Broadview to be with our boy. I think that sometimes, even when you know, there's some kind of mechanism deep inside that won't let you believe or imagine that something like this can happen to you or the people you love.

Stephen phoned me shortly before lunch and told me that the doctor there was having a hard time getting someone in Regina to see Kendall, and that we might have to go to Saskatoon. I'm not sure how I functioned through the rest of my shift. I was in the wrong place. Finally, a doctor in Regina agreed to see Kendall, so on their way to the city they stopped by my workplace to tell me what was happening. I remember going out to the truck. I gave Kendall a hug and told him everything would be fine, that I wasn't worried. You just never dream.

Not long after I got home from work, Stephen phoned. I couldn't understand what he was saying, and it took a while for me to realize that he was crying. Then I heard those words. "He has cancer." I couldn't breathe.

The doctor there removed the huge lump I had seen the night before to be biopsied, even though there was no doubt in his mind. It was just standard procedure. That night, Kendall returned to the hospital in Broadview, where they had him on heavy doses of antibiotics. Ativan, an anti-anxiety medication, was also prescribed, but he didn't want it. While he was understandably upset, he always believed he would get through it.

The next few days are foggy. I don't recall making Easter dinner. I'm sure I did, I always did. Shelley and all three children were here. I remember trying to keep things as light and as normal as possible. I think this is when I became a good actress, masking my true feelings and thoughts. Kendall would come home for the afternoon with the understanding that he had to be back in time for his meds. Elizabeth, in her attempt to keep things light, planned a birthday party for her dog, Milo. She had the kids sing Happy Birthday, and even bought gourmet dog food, in which she placed a candle. Did Milo eat this very special dog food? No.

How could this be happening? How could this be real? Where do we go from here? My beautiful, strong, athletic son, who made friends everywhere he went, had a horrible, life-threatening disease.

Shortly after six, Shelley and Elizabeth would drive Kendall back to the hospital. This was our routine for the next several days.

Over the next few weeks, we played the waiting game. I think because of his age and the type of cancer, his doctor was reluctant to perform the surgery, so he sent Kendall's file to a colleague in London, Ontario. You see,

Kendall was diagnosed with penile cancer, so the surgery would mean having a complete or partial penectomy at the age of 27. Stephen and I would have taken him to the ends of the earth, so a trip to Ontario was nothing, but all Kendall could see were dollar signs, and he didn't want to do that to us. In the end, it didn't matter. We got a call on a Monday, and his surgery was scheduled for Wednesday.

I was in close contact with my family, my mom phoned later that afternoon and I was so thankful she was flying here the next day. No matter how old we get, we will always need our moms, and I needed mine more than I had at any other time in my life.

Mom stayed for three weeks, and I can't even begin to tell you how helpful she was. It was at this time that I stopped sleeping. Falling asleep was easy, as long as I had the distraction of the television. Staying asleep was another story. Throughout the day, I couldn't sit, and had to be constantly busy and on the move. If I sat too long, my mind would take me places I just couldn't go. Kendall enjoyed having his grandmother here, not just because she baked him treats like homemade rolls and rhubarb crisps, but also because he loved her so much. As a small boy, he called her "Nanny," as did most of her grandchildren. As a young adult, he referred to her as Nanny when he was being playful and teasing her. During this time, he called her Nanny several times out of sadness over his loss and out of fear, not knowing what was to come. He always found such comfort in her.

One hour after the surgery, which only lasted a little over an hour, they brought Kendall to his room. None of us knew what to say or how to act. This was such a devastating loss for him, for any young man. I just wanted my baby boy to be well and healthy again. He had tears in his eyes and couldn't even muster a smile, although he did try, and I know it was for my sake. The first thing he said was, "Where's my Nanny?" She moved quickly to his side, kissed his cheek and said, "I'm right here." It was then that he let the tears flow, and my heart broke.

Physically, he recovered quickly.

One evening, the three of us were watching some silly program on TV. My husband had gone to bed earlier, when all of a sudden Kendall broke down. I tried so hard to comfort him. My mom started talking to him about the three beautiful children he did have, and about the possibility of reconstructive surgery. She finished it off by saying, "There are a lot of other ways to have sex." She calmed him down and he finally went off to bed. Before I did, I checked on him and, thankfully, he was sleeping. Some day, I will ask my mother to explain. I don't recall her ever talking to us about all the ways to have sex when we were growing up. Yet here she was, willing to share her knowledge with her grandson!

A few weeks later, Kendall was feeling well enough to go out with friends for the evening. He was always willing to talk about what was happening with his health if they asked. He even discussed going for reconstructive surgery in Alberta. He made it sound like shopping, and would jokingly say, "Does that one come in white?"

Mom was here to help us celebrate Kendall's 28th birthday, as were the kids. They spent time with us though most of Mom's visit. We had cake and sang, while he blew out his candles. We gave him a guitar, something he had mentioned he wanted. It was a good day.

Shortly after my mom left, my in-laws arrived. They were here in time for Kendall's second surgery, removal of lymph nodes on both sides of his groin. This surgery lasted four hours, followed by another two in recovery, and a truly horrible day. We knew it was going to be several hours before Kendall would be allowed visitors, so we left the hospital. My father-in-law bought lunch for everyone, and then we did some shopping. My heart and head were still in the hospital, wondering how Kendall was and what was happening.

We finally returned to the hospital and sat in a waiting room on the floor where we knew he would be placed. The minutes seemed to crawl by. I didn't speak; I had nothing to say. Nor did I have the desire to make small talk. Finally, we were given word that we could see him. He looked so small. His grandfather's eyes teared up, and he moved toward the window. Kendall only opened his eyes for a few moments, just long enough to know we were all there and for us to see he was okay. Beth took her grandparents back to our house shortly after that. Stephen and I stayed a while longer. Leaving him was always so hard. Kendall didn't bounce back from this surgery as quickly as he had from the first, and weight loss was becoming evident.

His children came for visits and enjoyed getting to know their great-grandparents. I was still not sleeping well at night, and throughout the days I always managed to find things to do to keep me moving.

Over the next several weeks, we all got to know the Regina Allan Blair clinic inside and out, as Kendall underwent chemo and radiation treatments. He stayed at the lodge through most of this time, as his radiation treatments needed to be done daily, and the hour and a half drive would have been too much. I hated leaving him when he needed me most. I would cry all the way home, even though he would tell me it was okay and say, "I'm a big boy Mom, I can do this. Don't worry." Of course, I did anyway. We would make the trip to the clinic whenever we could, and I phoned in between visits. Sometimes we would spend some time talking, other times he would be too sick from the chemo to come to the phone.

He had several friends living in the city who would come and kidnap him on his good days. One friend played in a rock band, so Kendall got to jam with them. I also remember once, while I was attending a workshop in Regina, I phoned Kendall when I finished for the day and the first thing he said was, "Please Mom, come break me out of here," so I did.

Finally, that round of treatments ended. Stephen and a family friend went to the city to pick him up. When he returned home, I noticed that he had purchased a new

MP3 player. He looked at me and said, "Don't say a word, I deserve this." He was right. He did deserve a new MP3 player and so much more. He didn't deserve to feel so tired all the time and unable to play with his boys or his daughter. My husband and I were always asking, "Why?" How did this become our reality? I think Stephen found it especially difficult. Working in Emergency Medical Services, he would see patients sick or dying on a daily basis because of addictions or drunken brawls. Where is the justice in any of this? I think it is only natural to question it when you see your child fighting for his life, and yet you see so many others with a total disregard for their own lives.

As summer was winding down, Kendall gained back some of the weight he had lost, and the sparkle was coming back into his eyes. He enjoyed playing with his children again, although he didn't have the stamina he used to. He went out with friends on the occasional evening, and even managed to go golfing a few times.

One of my sisters made the journey west for a visit that fall. She brought with her a quilt my mom had made for Kendall. He was so touched by this gift, and in awe of the attention he was getting from his family. I remember he even said to me once, "Are they coming just for me?" I smiled at him and said, "You are loved baby boy."

He was always so happy about the fact that he didn't lose his hair. It had thinned out a bit, but once I talked him into getting a cut he looked good and healthy.

In the fall he started another round of chemo and more radiation. He would get so sick from the chemo. It seemed like he would just start to feel better, and then it would be time for another treatment. There was one appointment that neither my husband nor I could get to, so Elizabeth made that journey with him. As they got closer to the city, he said to her, "I just don't want to, I get so sick. I don't want to." They spent the day shopping and had a nice lunch together. I'm glad they had such a good day.

Two of Stephen's brothers came next, and Kendall was thrilled. It still seemed so incredible to him that so many family members were making the trip. The week they were here, Kendall chose not to stay at the lodge while he was having radiation treatments, and his uncles assured him that they would take him there and back.

Both of his uncles were amazed by his strength and courage. On the last day of treatment, knowing that his cousin, the daughter of one of these uncles, would be coming to Regina with plans to begin training to become an RCMP officer, he drove his uncles to the RCMP barracks and toured the museum. He then gave them a tour of Regina, including the parliament buildings, after which he drove out of the city, he pulled off the highway and let his Uncle Glen drive home. When they arrived, they both had to help Kendall into the house. I could see they were visibly shaken, and at the same time so proud of him for the gift he had given them. Kendall's own thoughts that day were of his uncles, not of himself or his own discomfort. It was an afternoon they would look back on with fond memories.

Not long after this, another brother and sister of my husband's arrived, as well as a cousin from Alberta. Their goal was to take care of all of us. They only stayed a few short days, but each one in turn planned and cooked dinner, which was always so delicious. Kendall was feeling better for this visit, and was able to enjoy the meals as well as the many conversations he had with his aunt and uncle. Since it was November, they even planned a Christmas party, complete with gifts for all.

That December, Kendall was feeling back to his old self. His latest scan looked good, and his appetite was back. He started working at a local grocery store cutting meat. He never thought he would like that job but, being the consummate charmer and flirt that he was, he enjoyed all the older ladies that came in. He even went out to play hockey a few times with a rec team out of Broadview.

We had a really nice Christmas that year. Kendall went to McLean and spent Christmas Eve with Shelley and the children. She always extended this invitation so he could be there Christmas morning. He splurged and bought lobster for them. We always had seafood Christmas Eve. The boys have a picture of the three of them, all smiles, holding up these squirming creatures.

Kira was only three that year, and wanted a castle for Christmas. You can't be a princess and not have a castle. Kendall managed to find the exact one she wanted. For the boys, he got a foosball table. Kendall, being more boy than man when it came to Christmas, was so excited for his children to see those gifts. Those few days were filled with laughter, music and games. I wish it could have lasted longer.

A couple of weeks later, I was sitting in a chair by the living room window when I saw Kendall walking home from work. We only live a short distance from the store, he was moving so slowly, with a distinct limp. It took every bit of strength I could muster to fight back the tears. I didn't want him to see me cry. He ate very little supper that night and lay on the couch completely exhausted, watching TV with me. The next day, he phoned from work to see if his father could pick him up. He was leaving early, and knew he wouldn't be able to walk the few short blocks home.

Around this time, he underwent another cat scan. The doctor phoned and gave him the results, which I found unusual but still didn't question, and he was given an appointment for the following week. When we asked, of course he didn't tell us the truth. That night, however, I overheard him on the phone with my mom. My heart sank. I couldn't breathe. He must have misunderstood. Later, when I told my mom about this she said, "Yes, I just quit listening after I heard pancreas"

Early the next morning, I phoned the cancer clinic and insisted on an earlier appointment. We were given one for the next day. My next regret I didn't share any of what I had heard with my husband, and I should have. Looking back, I wish I had. For this appointment, Kendall needed a wheelchair. The walk from the front doors to the cancer clinic was just too far. When they called his name, I turned to my husband and said, "Are you coming?" His first response was "You don't need me." I gave him a long look, a look that only people who have been married a long time understand, and he said, "I guess I'm coming."

My husband and I made a good life for ourselves here in Saskatchewan. We raised two beautiful children and had three gorgeous grandchildren. We made the trip home several times over the years, had some amazing camping trips in various parks throughout the province, and while we had our share of hard times we were finally in a place where we could enjoy life and help our children. Kendall's dream was to be a teacher. He loved children, and already had his first year of schooling under his belt, so his father and I both planned to help him realize this dream.

So how did we get here, sitting in this doctor's office, hearing those awful words, six months to a year. This voice inside my head was screaming, *this is a nightmare how can this be real? You're talking about my son, mine!*

What do we do now? I don't want this to be us. I don't want these horrible circumstances to be ours. Not my boy, not my son. I felt lost. The ride home was quiet. None of us spoke. Looking back, I'm not even sure if the radio was on. We had spent a lot of time with the hospital counselors, and I think we were all talked out.

Small towns being what they are, this latest news traveled fast. Two friends stopped by that evening, and

Kendall actually went out with them for a bit. Stephen cooked supper that night, not that his cooking is unusual, more that I just didn't feel like eating. He brought my plate into the living room where I was sitting and said, "You should eat something." The next few weeks are a blur. I think I was in shock, and simply going through the motions of living.

Kendall got weaker. His limp became more and more pronounced, and he was tired most of the time. His meds were constantly being changed, in an effort to keep his pain under control. It seemed like we would fill a prescription on Friday and by Monday he would need something more, something stronger.

Friends in Indian Head organized a benefit in March, the funds from which were placed in a trust account for Kendall's children. It was a lovely evening. So many good friends came out, and Kendall felt so honored that people would do this for him. He was only able to stay a short time and as he was trying to sneak away people noticed and gave him a standing ovation. As long as I live I'll never forget that moment, the look on his face, or how I felt.

By now I had stopped working altogether. I needed to be home with Kendall.

Kendall with Nanny, the boys and Beth,
the end of her visit 2004.

Kendall with Brendan, Randy and Kira
Photo courtesy of Paper Moon Photography.

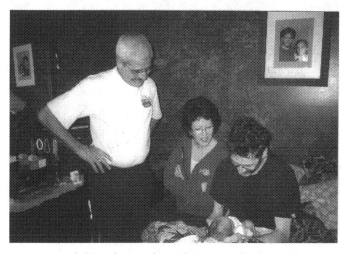

Kendal Stephen and I with Jazmin the day Beth
brought her home from the Hospital.

*Kendall, Brendan, Randy and Kira at Kendall's
surprise Birthday party, May 2005.*

Chapter 7

There are a lot of important points I have left out so far. The guitar we gave to Kendall, he learned to play through lessons given to him by his sister as a gift on that same birthday, and through the use of the internet. He spent hours practicing in the basement, and then he would come upstairs and make me stop whatever I was doing to listen to him play.

I would be flicking through the TV channels and he would say "Simpsons, Simpsons, Simpsons," to this day, I can still hear his voice as I change the channels. Day after day, week after week, I would go downstairs to give him his meds and breakfast, and he would be watching *Independence Day*. He could recite the dialogue from the entire movie. Today, it's the only Sci Fi movie that makes me cry. Once, when I went downstairs, he was watching *Godzilla*, so I asked if *Independence Day* was broken and he just laughed and said, "No." At bed time on the nights the kids were here, Kendall would always ask, "So what movie are we watching tonight?" and Kira would always shout, "*Bug's Life*!" The boys of course would groan, "Not again," and we would assure them that she would be fast asleep in no time, and they would be able to watch something else.

There were times when I held Kendall as he cried but, as I said, he was a lot like me. He always appeared so brave, and no one ever heard him ask, "Why me?"

In April of 2005, Elizabeth gave us a beautiful granddaughter, Jazmin Peach. When they came home from the hospital, they stayed with us for a few days, and we do have several pictures of her snuggled up in her Uncle Kendall's arms. Beth decided to stay as she wanted to be there with us and her brother.

Kendall was becoming weaker, and he spent more time sleeping. I was always so happy on those rare days when he would pick up his guitar. For his 29th birthday, Elizabeth and I planned a surprise party. We invited some of his closest friends, and of course his children were here. All that day I kept saying, "Why don't you go jump in the shower, you'll feel better." He kept saying, "Later, before bed." One by one his friends showed up, and it took him a while to clue in. Finally I looked at him and said, "Surprise!" His response: "If I had known, I would have showered."

Shortly after his birthday, the decision was made to have another round of chemo to try and shrink some of the tumors, to try and buy more time and control the pain. Kendall agreed to this, as long as it was a different mix. After a couple of weeks and an MRI, they could see there was no change, so Kendall chose not to continue and wanted to come home.

After being so proud of the fact that he hadn't lost his hair, now he was. I went into his room on a Saturday morning and it was coming out in huge clumps. I went back to the living room, sat on the couch and cried openly. He stared at me and asked, "What? Why are you crying? It's just hair." I couldn't answer. I just knew my heart was breaking.

In early July, at another doctor's appointment, it was decided that he would have a few more radiation treatments. He had a tumor pressing on his spine, could barely walk upright and was in a lot of pain. He was reluctant at first, but finally agreed, another hospital stay, I hated it. I didn't want to leave him, and I knew he just wanted to be home.

His cousin Heidi came for a visit during this time. Even though they grew up miles apart, they managed to remain close. Heidi spent every afternoon and evening with Kendall in the hospital. She was such a big help. There were a couple of days when I was too exhausted to go, and I felt quite comfortable knowing she was taking my place. He finally finished his treatment, so Heidi and Elizabeth drove into the city to pick him up. They made a stop at a hobby shop, and Kendall bought two models for the boys, thinking they would work on them together. One was a model of an aircraft carrier, but I can't for the life of me remember what the other one was. He teased Heidi that night about how he was glad she was with him with her long blond hair and short skirt. That way no one would notice him with his bald head sitting in a wheelchair. Those models still are tucked away under Brendan's bed; they never did get to work on them. Hopefully some day, the boys will put them together, maybe when they are older.

Brendan, Randy and Kira were here again, and they had so much fun with Heidi. She spent a lot of time playing with them in the pool we had in our back yard. She would take pictures and run into the house to show Kendall, as he rested in his room. The window faced the back yard, so he could hear all the giggles and laughter. Heidi, being a nurse, took over my role, and made sure that Kendall took his meds on time and that he ate something, even if it was only several small meals. Being a nurse who had worked with so many cancer patients, Heidi was also very aware of where we were, time-wise. As Kendall's mother, so was I. His father still held onto hope, couldn't bring himself to believe. Elizabeth, my sweet baby girl, was trying to be everyone's rock, my shoulder to lean on. I know I wasn't there for her over those months. At the end of the day, I had nothing left to give.

Not long after Heidi left, Kendall returned to the hospital in Broadview. He had many stays there, so he knew and cared for all the nurses and they cared for him in return. This time I refused to leave, so they gave me a roll-out bed for his room. I remember that first afternoon. I was watching him sleep when he woke up, and this little smile came over his face when he saw me sitting there. I asked him what he was smiling about and he said, "Nothing. It's just nice waking up and seeing you there."

My parents and two of my sisters were coming next. I spoke with my sister Susan several times to get an exact date as to when they were leaving, since I knew they were driving and that it would take them a few days. During one of our conversations I started to cry, and all I could say was, "Please hurry. Please, Susan, you need to hurry." I cared for my baby boy for months. I watched him leave us bit by bit, piece by piece, and I knew even though I didn't want to know. I knew we were running out of time. I also knew I wasn't strong enough to go through it just the three of us. I, we needed as much family as possible here to help us get through what would come next.

On a Sunday, the day my parents should have arrived, Kendall had a truly good day. The best he had had in a long time. The day was sunny and warm, and Kendall was actually sitting up on the couch watching his favorite show. Yes, *The Simpsons.* We ordered burgers and fries from a local restaurant, and Kendall ate more than I had seen him eat in a very long time. Stephen was at work and out on a call, Elizabeth was here with her boyfriend and Jazmin, and we all had such a good afternoon talking and laughing. He was Kendall again, with a big full laugh, the kind that starts way down in your belly, and his eyes shone. Okay, that might have been the morphine. Still, it felt so good to sit beside him, talking and laughing and enjoying a good burger. If only I could have that moment back again.

Sadly, Sunday turned out to be Kendall's last good day: my family arrived the day after. My sister Anna Marie was the first to go into the living room where

Kendall was positioned on the couch to say hello. She came back to the kitchen in tears and whispered, "How can you stand it? How do you do it?" I told her in a voice stronger than I felt, "Because he's my son, and I love him."

There is no love greater than that of a mother for her child. My mind takes be back to days past, the little boy, eager to ride a two-wheeler, raking leaves into a pile and seeing out of the corner of my eye a mischievous boy ready to run and dive in. Mother's Day, one in particular, always comes to mind. Both of my children served me breakfast in bed: burnt toast covered in hard margarine, soggy Cheerios and instant coffee. I recall Kendall asking if the coffee was okay. "I wasn't sure how to make it Mommy. I put four teaspoons in, is that right? Is it good?" Having both of my babies, standing by my bed, eyes gleaming with huge smiles on their faces, I told them it was perfect and drank every drop.

The young man of 17, who played with all the young children on our street after school to keep them safe the year a young child nearly drowned, when the creek beside our home filled beyond capacity.

How did we get here? If everything in life happens for a reason, what is the reason for this? Most families travel life's highways with only a few bumps in the road. Why not my family? I don't want to do this. Sometimes I wonder what would happen if I walked out the door and just kept walking. Of course I don't, I can't.

Sometimes I would dream about what the future would be like when I grow old. Elizabeth would be in charge of family dinners, we would all be there. Elizabeth with her family, perhaps even with grandchildren. Kendall would be there with his wife. Brendan and Randy would be there with their own small children running around and, of course, Kira would be there. I had pictured, in my mind's eye, Kendall stopping by to check on me the way my dad did with his mom. Isn't this the way it's supposed to be? Not like this. Children aren't supposed to leave this earth before their parents.

At the end of the day, I do believe there is a higher power with a different plan, yet I just can't help but question, *Why my son? I have only one. He is my heart. Why my heart?*

Chapter 8

My mom went next to say hello, and to give him one of her famous bear hugs that he loved so much and always asked for. My dad came into the room and touched Kendall's shoulder and said, "Hello man." I could see that his heart was breaking. I felt torn in so many directions, and my daughter, I knew she was in pain. She kept her emotions in check, held everything inside, waiting to burst. I didn't have the energy to help her. My parents, I can't stand to see them hurting, and I know they feel the same. Stephen, my husband of 29 years and I held each other when we cried, but I didn't have to speak. I only had enough energy to focus on my son. I've never felt so tired. I didn't want to do this. I wanted my life back. The way things used to be. I wanted to sing and dance with my baby boy.

The next day was quiet. It was August 2, Kira's birthday. Kendall ate and drank very little that day. I only managed to get him to drink enough to get his meds down, and to eat a little soup. I could see this was very upsetting to my parents and my sisters. However, no one mentioned it or questioned it.

My mom made me a scrapbook all about Kendall. It's so beautiful, and it's easy to see she put a tremendous amount of work into it. She thought that I would be in tears immediately, and both of my sisters watched me carefully as I took my time going through the pages. By this time I was beyond exhaustion. I had already shed so many tears, and my whole body felt the weight of my sadness. Having them here with me, with us, was such a relief. I knew I would need them to hold me up and give me the strength I would need to get through what I knew was coming.

The next day, Kendall was a little more alert. I managed to get him to the table for breakfast, and my sister Anna Marie got him talking and distracted enough that he ate some of his porridge and took his meds. Suddenly, he looked up at me and told me I should phone Kira. When I asked him why, he said because it's her birthday. That was yesterday. When I told him the date he started to cry. I put my arms around him and told him that it was okay. The kids were coming down soon and we were planning a birthday party for her. I knew it didn't help. It wasn't just missing his baby girl's birthday; it was losing an entire day.

My sister Susan decided she would make homemade vegetable soup for Kendall. She thought if only he would eat, he would feel better. Both of my sisters tried hard to feed my baby boy. It was so sweet, and I knew they just wanted to do something to help him. I felt very comfortable leaving Kendall in their capable hands while I escaped to the back yard.

One afternoon, I was outside working in my flower garden. On one of my trips inside to see how they were making out, I saw that my sisters had Kendall sitting up on the couch, one on either side, and they were feeding him. They were talking to each other, and Kendall would look from one to the other as each one in turn placed a spoonful of soup into his mouth. I stood there watching for a few moments and for some unknown reason I found the whole thing rather comical. I started to laugh and said all that was missing was the crown on top of Kendall's head. While I had my sisters' attention, I noticed Kendall pushing away his main meal and reaching for the rhubarb crisp that Mom had made, and this made me laugh even harder. He flashed my sisters one of his famous goofy grins, and all they could do was shake their heads and smile.

This memory is so special to me. I could see the love and caring between all three of them, and it meant so much to Kendall not only that his aunts had made the trip to see him, but also that they loved him so much that they wanted to take care of him.

Later, during a conversation with my sister Susan, I found out that she did some research on death and dying when she returned home, and learned that people who are close to death usually have no interest in food. It had been so important to her to make that soup for Kendall and to make sure he ate it, that she now felt silly. We both shed more than a few tears at that memory. Kendall was so touched that she cared that much, and every time I go back to that memory, I smile through my tears. Mom's rhubarb crisp was the last thing Kendall had to eat.

Chapter 9

U p to this point, there are a few things I have left out of the story that I will share with you now. Caring for someone with cancer is a difficult thing, especially when it's someone you love, especially when it's your child. Kendall had so much medication right from the start, all with a different purpose. This one you take before you eat, this one for the side effects of that one, this one for pain and so on and so on. That part was easy. Not being able to sleep at night without the television on because of all the places my mind would wander; even today this is still my practice.

The mornings I would find him on the floor, when he had tried to get up but couldn't. He wouldn't call out because he didn't want to wake us. Unless you have been there, you have no idea how difficult it is to see your child, who was always such a strong athlete, unable to pick himself up off the floor, never mind getting there in the first place.

Living moment by moment, baby step by baby step, not wanting to go anywhere, even just to the neighbor's for coffee, because any time spent away is time you'll never get back.

Having this constant scream living inside you, afraid to let it out for fear you'll never stop. Wanting to hold tight and not being able to because he still needs his space. Wanting to ask what he's thinking but not really wanting an answer. The things you are imagining in your own mind are enough. Watching him while he watched his children. As soon as Kendall moved upstairs, so did his children. They took over the living room. I gave them blankets and pillows, and they positioned themselves on the floor in front of the TV. From his vantage point, Kendall would be more focused on them than whatever movie was playing. I would sit and watch him watch them, and I could see his eyes glistening with tears, and every now and then he would brush one away. No, I never asked what he was thinking or feeling. I couldn't. He was always a lot like me, wearing his heart on his sleeve. Most of the time, I could read him like a book. Elizabeth has always been just like her Dad. Kendall was always my other me.

Chapter 10

Not long after Elizabeth had Jazmin, they came home. By this time Kendall could no longer make it up and down the stairs. In the beginning, he said it was because the bed in the spare room was more comfortable than his. Of course, I knew this wasn't the case, since the beds were purchased only one month apart and were exactly the same.

Elizabeth would come upstairs at 3 A.M. to warm a bottle for Jazmin, and she could hear Kendall quietly calling for her. She would take him juice or make him instant porridge and they would spend a few moments, just the two of them, talking quietly into the wee hours of the morning. I believe she needed to be home to spend that time with him. Later on she told me that during the day he was mine, but late at night he was hers. She continued this ritual, even through Kendall's final stay at the Broadview Hospital.

On Friday, August 5, Brendan, Randy and Kira came to our house and as planned we had a small birthday party for Kira. Elizabeth had gone shopping for Kendall, who by this time was in a hospital bed in our living room. He slept through most of the day, only stirring long enough for Kira to show him her gifts. That evening, Stephen set the tent up in the back yard for him and the boys to sleep in. We tried so hard to keep things as normal as possible for them. I had slept in a chair by Kendall's bed the night before, and his breathing was so bad. The cancer had already moved to his lungs. Once Stephen and the kids were settled in the tent, I lay on our bed and crashed. I'm not sure how long I slept. It was my Mom who came to wake me, telling me that Kendall was calling for me. I rushed to the living room. He said he needed the bathroom, but in the end it was just me that he needed. I sat with him for a long time.

The next morning, Stephen and I helped him into the bathroom. I bathed him and helped him dress. As we were laying him back into bed, he couldn't breathe. We quickly sat him up again, and the panic in his eyes tore at my heart. We are supposed to be able to fix everything for our children and we couldn't fix this. That voice that kept screaming inside my head was getting louder. *Please, someone help me! I don't want to do this! Help me wake up from this nightmare! Not my son. Please, not my baby boy.*

Kendall went by ambulance to the hospital. His children, grandparents and aunts looked on as our friends (my husband's co-workers) loaded him into the back of the unit.

The nurses kept Kendall sedated, which in truth was what we wanted. I couldn't bear to see him in pain. We played music in his room, including some of his favorites like AC/DC and Metallica. I knew he was aware of what was going on around him just by some of the expressions on his face. We played a CD that he had purchased on one of our trips home to New Brunswick, and he had tears rolling down his cheeks. That CD always reminded us of home.

My husband and I both stayed at the hospital with Kendall. Elizabeth would drive down in the wee hours and sit with him while we slept. I caught her once, and asked why she was here. She just said she couldn't sleep. It was just the four of us again, like it was when the kids were small. All the Christmases, Mother's Days, Father's Days, and all the special days when it was just the four of us.

I don't want to do this. That voice was getting louder.

The next day, when the nurses were turning Kendall, he woke up and wanted to see his children. Mom and Susan had arrived at the hospital, so Stephen and I drove home to Grenfell to pick them up. I took this opportunity to try and quiet my mind. I showered and changed, then told the boys that their Dad wanted to see them. Shelley had picked up Kira earlier, so Beth went to McLean to bring her back. Brendan sat on the couch, and I remember he looked so sad. He looked at me and said, "Grammie, I don't want to." He was so young and all of this was so unfair, but I knew he needed to do this so I sat down beside him and very honestly told him, "Brendan, I don't want to do this either but I love him so I'm doing it." Weeks later, Brendan told me that he was glad he went.

I remember sitting in the waiting room with my sister Susan. She was holding me and I was crying. I kept asking her, how is it possible to want someone to go and stay all at the same time. I loved him so much, my baby boy, my heart. How am I supposed to live without my heart?

That night, my husband and I were sitting outside while the nurses attended to Kendall. When we returned to his room, there were two extra beds, one for each of us. They had placed a chocolate on our pillows and there was a fresh pot of coffee. I can't even begin to tell you how much I love these women. They are nurses in every sense of the word.

The next day was August 11. The weather had changed. We awoke to overcast skies and the threat of rain. My parents and Susan arrived shortly before noon. I was surprised to see my Dad. He didn't always come. I think he found it too hard. Everything happens for a reason, where we are is where we are supposed to be.

They hadn't been there long when Kendall woke up. He was very agitated, and in a lot of pain. I ran to get the nurse so she could increase his morphine, however, this time it didn't work.

Stephen's father and one of his brothers were on their way, and I kept thinking they would be here at any moment and someone should stop them at the desk. I didn't want them walking into the room without being prepared.

Everything seemed to be happening so fast, yet moving in slow motion. His doctor came into the room, but only for a moment. Dad had moved to the waiting room. Stephen was on one side of the bed, I on the other, my mom by my side. I remember looking up and seeing that the door was closed. The realization of what was happening hit me like a hammer. The voice in my head was screaming so loud I couldn't hear anything else. I climbed onto the bed, held him close and whispered in his ear all the things I knew he needed to hear. I told him how very much I loved him, how very much his family loved him. I said to him, "You will always be my hero for your strength and courage, and for all the things you taught us about what is truly important in life. You have fought long and hard, and it's okay to let go. We will miss you and love you always, and your Grammie Ruth is waiting for you." I kissed his cheek and, a few moments later, he was gone.

Kendall and Heidi at the end of her visit July 2005.

Kendall, Heidi and Myself,
these were the last photos taken of Kendall, July 2005

Kendall, Heidi and Kira, July 2005.

Chapter 11

So many moments from that last hour are forever burned into my memory. To this day, when one of those moments makes its way to the surface, I can't breathe.

Kendall was holding tight to my hand and I to his, when all of a sudden I felt this need to run. My sister Susan gave me this look, questioning whether I was okay. I shook my head, placed his hand in hers and ran. I found myself outside, racing around the back yard of the hospital. I couldn't breathe. That voice kept screaming, *I can't, I can't, I don't want to, I don't want to!* I finally managed to get those thoughts under control and return to my baby boy's side, taking his hand from my sister. I'm sure the nursing staff was aware, and my mom later told me that she was made aware through discussions she had had with a counselor she had been seeing throughout Kendall's illness. Neither myself nor my husband, however, realized what that last hour would be like.

Kendall had told us months before that there were three things he wanted. One was his guitar, and it did bring him so much joy. Another was to go easy. This was not to be. At one point, he reached up and grabbed his father's shirt and twisted it in his hand. He begged his father, "Please help me, Dad." He was in so much pain, and there was nothing his dad could do. For my husband, as you can imagine, this is his most painful memory.

I remember the look on my daughter's face when she arrived too late. I'm so sorry baby girl. Although everything seemed to be happening in slow motion, there was little time to think. Beth raced to the hospital at a dangerously fast speed and flew into his room, only to be told by her dad, "He's gone."

We sat for a long time by his bed. I remember I kept touching his face, stroking his head and adjusting his blankets. Stephen finally left the room, and when I looked up I noticed my mom was still standing by my side. I said to her "You stayed," and through her own tears she simply answered, "You did."

I left then to go and find Stephen. He was sitting in the courtyard. We sat together crying, not speaking, lost in our own thoughts. My mom and Susan gathered all the things from Kendall's room, getting ready to leave the hospital for the last time. Stephen, Elizabeth and I sat with Kendall for a while longer, holding onto each other and saying our own quiet goodbyes. We then left the room, closing the door behind us.

The service was quite beautiful, for what it was. I had asked my sister if she would speak, and her initial response was "No." Then the next day, when she was walking by my bedroom on her way to shower, she came in and said she changed her mind. Her reason, she said, was that if Kendall could do what he did and face it all with such strength, grace and dignity, then she could do this. To this day, when she is faced with something hard, she thinks of Kendall and forges ahead.

Stephen's brother Glenn also spoke, as did three of Kendall's friends and his high school principal. It was important to me that the people who spoke knew him well, and that the service be a celebration of his life. I knew he would like that.

A few days later, we loaded up the jeep and headed home to New Brunswick.

Chapter 12

The third thing that Kendall had wanted was to go home. I had found plane tickets at a very good price for Kendall, all three children and myself, thinking that Stephen and Elizabeth would follow. This was not to be. We would have to leave mid-May, and the boys were still in school. Shelley wasn't too sure if she wanted to take them out early, even though I assured her that my sister Anna Marie, who is a teacher, would help them with their remaining school work. In the end, Kendall decided we should wait until school finished and I didn't push the issue any further, even though I knew it would be too late by then.

Of the three things he wanted, I only had control over one of them. I'm so glad we gave him that guitar. God had control over the first thing, how he left us, and Kendall himself had control over the third.

We stayed in New Brunswick for almost a month. It was good to be with family, allowing them to take care of us. I couldn't help but think that this was supposed to be our trip. Kendall had wanted to be home so badly, and we had talked about making the trip often, the people he wanted to see and the places he wanted to visit. Choices.

On a warm sunny day, Stephen, Elizabeth and I went for a drive to my in-laws' cottage. Kendall loved this place, canoeing on the river or just taking in all the sights and sounds of nature. We took some of his ashes with us. He would like always being a part of this place, a place he loved and longed to be. We sat on the deck for a long time enjoying the sun and just watching the river, each of us lost in our own thoughts.

Saying goodbye is always hard, but it was time to get going. Stephen had to be back at work, and we missed the boys and Kira.

How is a person just supposed to step back into their life? I really don't know the answer. My husband went back to work when we returned, and I'm not sure how he managed to do that, especially the first time he had to go to the hospital in Broadview and into room 13, the last place our son had stayed.

I did not hurry back to work. Everything seemed too hard: visiting with friends, going shopping, even just going for a walk. I loved spending time with Beth and Jazmin, but I do believe Jazmin could sense my sadness, and neither one of us was comfortable being alone together. I felt bad about that. I just didn't have it in me to be solely responsible for this little person.

Months later, Jazzy (as we would come to call her) became our saving grace. Whenever we were feeling really low, we would phone for Jazzy to come and visit. Almost immediately, our moods would change. How could they not? She is such a happy, loving child, with a head full of soft brown curls, so much like her mother's. I don't think we would have made it through that first year if it wasn't for her, and I often wonder if she is aware of the weight she carries, even now, on her small shoulders. Some day she will know.

I stopped doing a lot of the things that I used to do. My flower garden no longer brought me pleasure, most likely because I spent so much time there escaping from the reality of my life. Friends that I used to see almost daily, I had no time for. I had no desire to listen to stories of everyday events, especially stories of their sons, when my whole world as I knew it was gone. Even simple things, like going to the grocery store it was almost two years before I could go there without having a panic attack.

Christmas luckily came and went, as it always does. So many tears. New Years was even more difficult. All I could think was, "Oh my God, Kendall doesn't exist in this year."

I slowly started back to work, just a few hours at a time. Stephen and I spent a lot of time ice fishing that first winter. I would sit there with my line in the hole, the warm sun on my face and the quiet of the valley and suddenly I would realize I was smiling. Kendall's children came with us a few times. I would pack sandwiches, cookies and, of course, hot chocolate. I remember this one time in particular, the sandwiches were gone and the thermos was empty. Kira came over to where I was sitting, her little hands on her hips, and said to me, "Grammie, I don't know why you're having fun, 'cause I'm not." My husband and I both started to laugh and at the same time said, "Well, I guess it's time to go."

Through work, long before Kendall became ill, I became actively involved with my union, so upon my return I picked up where I had left off. These activities kept my mind occupied and I still enjoy that work today.

Chapter 13

I was working hard to keep busy trying to fill every moment of my days. So many small things would catch me off guard: a song from that summer, silly advertisements, even the Simpsons. Oddly enough, we didn't watch that show for over a year.

Stephen and I sought out grief counseling, which we did find helpful. In fact we are still in contact with a couple whom we met there.

One day in February, I was having a particularly hard day. I felt this need to do something. I kept thinking, 'Kendall was here, he was loved, please remember.' I had heard about the Canadian Cancer Society's Relay for Life event through family in New Brunswick, so I decided to give them a call.

Within a few days, representatives from the society came out to meet with us and help us get started. I had organized some of my friends and they in turn brought more friends. In total, about twenty-five of us showed up for the presentation. They explained how Relay began, all the different ceremonies, and how even they were surprised at the response this event had received clear across the country. Originally, they thought it would be a city event. The society was a little shocked and pleased when so many rural communities wanted to take on this event.

Then they showed us a very moving and powerful PowerPoint presentation. Images of cancer survivors and families mixed with music, and just the sight of so many people coming together to celebrate and to remember was very emotional. There wasn't a dry eye in the house. One woman in attendance had just recently been diagnosed with breast cancer and it had only been a few months since we had lost Kendall and of course, everyone there had their own story. Afterwards, they asked us if we were truly interested in hosting the event and everyone said yes. I was sitting there, this ridiculous grin on my face, trying so hard to hold it together and I could hear my friends saying, "I'll do food!" "I'll do teams!" "I'll look after volunteers!" Then one of the CCS reps said, "You'll need an event chair. Will one of you take that on?" My friends all responded, "Marilyn. She is our event chair," and so it began. I don't think any of us were aware of the enormity of the project we were taking on. We just dove in determined to make it work, to make it successful.

Elizabeth was the volunteer chair that year. She spoke with every group organization and retired person within our community until she compiled a list of names that she felt was adequate. I took on the role of entertainment chair and sponsorship co-chair, as well as event chair.

I know Stephen worried about me during this time. If I wasn't working on Relay, then I was doing union business, filling every moment of every day. He was also very aware that I wasn't sleeping. I would fall down into bed by eleven-thirty or twelve, and would be up by four or "the middle of the night," as he referred to it. I just kept telling him, "Don't worry. I will sleep after Relay."

I was on a mission, not just for myself but also for the people in my community. So many had been affected by this disease, you don't pay attention. You just don't know until you become one of them: until you all have the same story.

One afternoon over lunch, when it was time to get our own team registered and start fundraising, we were trying to come up with a team name. We tossed around several ideas, but none of them seemed quite right. Lisa, a good family friend and someone who loved Kendall looked up from her plate and said, "Cheeky Monkey." Beth and I both said through our tears, "Yes, that is our name." That was the name Kendall had affectionately called his daughter. We were Team Cheeky Monkey.

The week before Mother's Day that year, Beth was getting ready to move into a home of her own. She spent most of that week painting and trying to pack. I was at her house on the Saturday before Mother's Day helping her with Jazzy, and with some final touches, when Stephen showed up. I could see that he was upset. All he would say was that I needed to come home there was something I needed to see. Naturally I thought it was a gift from him, since he always got me something for Mother's Day. I was wrong. I walked into my living room, and there on the coffee table was a beautiful bouquet of pink flowers. I looked at him and was about to say thank you when I noticed he had tears in his eyes. All he could say was, "They're not from me." It was a beautiful arrangement of flowers, all pink. Pink daisies, pink tulips, and one tiny pink rose with bits of baby's breath throughout. Attached to the card was an angel on my shoulder pin - pink. The card simply said, "Thank you Mom love Kendall." Just then the phone rang; it was my sister Anna Marie. I see her still, sitting in a chair pulled close to Kendall's bed, pen and paper in hand. Kendall by this time was so weak and tired that he spoke in a whisper. She helped him to write letters for each of his children, being patient, giving him time to get the words out, knowing he only had strength to write one letter but personalizing it for each child. I see her still, leaning in, talking softly, thinking all the while "What a wonderful gift you are giving, my son," without any knowledge of the gift I would receive. Kendall asked her if she would send me flowers, all pink. He told her pink flowers were my favorite. She went through all the holidays, and he would shake his head no, until she finally landed on Mother's Day and he nodded his head yes. She then asked what the card should say. My baby boy loved me enough that he wanted me to have this lovely bouquet of flowers and he wanted to say thank you. As much as I missed my son, in that moment I knew he had left this earth feeling completely loved by his family and in the end that's all that matters.

The day of the relay finally arrived. I was nervous and excited all at the same time. As event chair, I had planned to speak. I couldn't, in the end, I think it was just too soon. All the planning and preparation doesn't prepare you. This event is charged with so much emotion. Unless you experience it for yourself, you just can't know. As the survivors were making their way around the track, I felt this huge lump rise up in my throat and I had to walk away. Both Brendan and Randy came to find me, slipped their arms around my waist and said, "I wish Daddy was wearing a yellow shirt." As hard as I tried, I couldn't hold back my tears. I whispered to them both, "Me too." We raised over sixty-four thousand dollars that year. I was on a high. It felt so good knowing I had a small part in raising that much money, that I helped so many people gain knowledge and find support. I couldn't wait to start planning the next one.

We began planning our next relay in October. New committee members joined our team with fresh enthusiasm and ideas. Beth took on the role of luminary chair. I was still event chair as well as entertainment chair. We chose June 1 as the date for our event, and no one sitting around the table except Beth was aware of the fact that June 1 is my birthday. Beth smiled at me from across the table but didn't say anything. Nor did I.

It was a sunny, warm, beautiful day. Like the previous year, we worked all day setting up, making sure we had enough tables, getting all the luminaries around the track, all the final preparations for an event this size. For this event, I did speak as part of the opening ceremonies. I practiced my speech every spare moment I found that day, and not once did I get through it. When the time came for me to take the stage, I thought my heart would pound out of my chest. My hands were shaking, and I was grateful that I had most of my speech memorized, since I could barely see the words. That year, we used a wagon for the survivors that could not walk the track and as they finished their victory lap, the wagon ended up parked in front of stage. I took the microphone and turned toward the audience, and there directly in front of me, seated in the wagon, was an elderly gentleman proudly wearing his yellow shirt. He had these wonderfully kind eyes, a smile on his lips, arms folded across his chest, patiently waiting for me to begin. All the while I spoke, I looked directly at him and some of my nerves faded away. I spoke of the survivors' victory lap and how they are our hope. I talked about Kendall, not only about how much we missed him, but also about everything he had taught us about love and life. As I ended my speech, this wonderful, gentle man closed his eyes and nodded, his smile spreading across his face. This has to be the reason. Everything my baby boy went through this has to be the reason. So many people heard my message. So many people came up to me that night with kind words and hugs. Some had no words at all, just huge hugs. Two short years before, I never would have dreamed I would be standing on a stage, sharing my story, giving hope and support to so many. If everything in life happens for a reason, could this be the reason why my son and my family have gone through all that we have?

As the luminary ceremony began, I could hear Ryan, Kendall's childhood friend, playing the bagpipes as we bent to light candles to honor and remember my sweet baby boy. I kept thinking, 'I will share your story, a story of strength, courage and grace. I will share our story, and hopefully bring comfort and support to whoever will listen.' Though I didn't know it at the time, a group of women had come together as a Relay team, each one of them a breast cancer survivor, and out of their team meetings they ended up forming a support group. How wonderful is that?

Our third Relay was in Indian Head, with a new chair at the helm. Beth and I joined this new committee as luminary co-chairs. This was the year Relay saw some changes, with three new ceremonies: Celebrate, Remember, Fight Back. I couldn't have been more pleased. We took all the ideas we learned at summit which we attended earlier in the year and ran with it. Being luminary co-chairs meant that the Remember Ceremony was ours. How fitting. I had felt that the luminary ceremony was too small, and that it didn't give people the time they needed to go through all of their emotions. The new format made it so much more. An important change, at least to me, is that we now take the time to honor all of the caregivers, a role I knew all too well.

This was also the first year we personalized our team t-shirts, using our own family photos. My husband chose a picture of himself and Kendall sitting on the bench at a slow pitch tournament. Brendan's was a photo of him and his dad putting a telescope together that last Christmas. Kira's was a photo of her dad kissing her cheek, and Randy chose a picture of his dad teaching him guitar. Beth chose a photo of her and her brother in New Brunswick. Jazmin's photo was taken the day she came home from the hospital, one of only a few we have of her snuggled in her uncle's arms. Mine was a picture of me with my arms wrapped around my baby boy. We all proudly wore our team shirts, letting everyone know that we were there to remember our son, our brother, our father, our uncle, and that we were fighting back for him.

When I first made that initial phone call to the Canadian Cancer Society, I had no idea how important this event would become, how much it would mean to me. It truly is so much more than just a fundraiser. It is a night when we can all come together and share our stories. It is the one night I can talk about my baby boy and its okay. To quote myself from one of my last speeches, "When you laugh, we all laugh. When you cry, we all cry - because we know."

Our Relay Team, Cheeky Monkeys.

Brendan, Randy and Myself in our Relay shirts.

The Aftermath

Five years. Summer, August… So many things can happen in five years. So many things *have* happened. I'm slowly finding my way back to enjoying summer again, although everything about summer still takes me back. I've simply decided that's not a bad thing.

Brendan will turn seventeen this fall, and is working the summer as a lifeguard. Randy has grown so tall for thirteen and will soon tower over his older brother. Kira will soon be nine. Her missing teeth were replaced with adult teeth, and every time she comes to visit she measures herself to me; not yet baby girl. Kendall would be so proud.

In August of 2006, we started what would become our annual camping trip, a chance for us all to get away together. The first night, sitting around the fire, we share stories of their dad. I'm finding, now that they are older, that they want more than just to hear stories. They want to know their dad, what he was like. They enjoy hearing how open he was to making new friends, and how he flirted with the ladies who came into the grocery store but mostly they love hearing how very much he loved them.

We lost Stephen's mom in 2007, followed a short year later by his dad. Beth shared with me a dream she had shortly after her grandfather's funeral. We all came home and were heading to her grandparents' camp on the Tobique River. She said we looked across to where the camp is situated and there, sitting on the swing as if waiting for us, were her grandparents and her brother. She found her dream upsetting, I think because this was just too many losses for her. I liked the idea that all three were in a place that they loved, and I believe they are waiting for us and will be there when the time comes.

This year, just a little over a year after losing my father-in-law, we suffered another loss, my Dad, too many losses in such a short time. Dad was a man of few words, and yet he was this huge presence in our family, and we all knew by his actions how much he loved us. One of my favorite things had been listening to my dad sing and play guitar. I will miss him always.

Beth gave us another granddaughter, Grace Elizabeth, named after my mom. She is such a chubby little thing, with soft curly hair and huge blue eyes. Our family is changing, growing.

As for myself, I feel like I'm a work in progress. I started taking guitar lessons. Replacing the strings on Kendall's guitar was very difficult. It's funny how it's always the little things that get you. The strings were so worn out and it needed to be done, but all I kept thinking was that his fingers had played those strings.

I joined a group called the Grenfell Community Players, putting on dinner theatres how crazy is that? Me, on stage, performing. Me, always so shy and quiet, prancing around the stage in fishnet stockings in front of hundreds of people! I think Kendall would be proud.

We are still very much involved with Relay and making plans to bring it back to Grenfell for 2011.

My husband started bow hunting. I think he enjoys the quiet and solitude. His efforts have certainly paid off. I now have a seven-foot bear standing in my dining room. Hopefully now he has the incentive to redo the basement, so that his prize can have a new home.

We still speak of Kendall often, determined to keep his memory alive. There are still times when tears flow freely and other times when we laugh so hard that we cry. I will also be honest in saying that I still have moments when the full realization of it hits me and I can't breathe. I have just decided, though, that that's okay.

He was here, he was loved, and I will always remember.